Of Bushmen and Brumbies

Rhythms of the Bush

Helen Iles

All rights reserved. No part of this publication may be reproduced, stored in a retrieval system, or transmitted in any form or by any means, electronic, mechanical, photocopying or otherwise, without the prior written permission of the Publishers.

First published 2013 Paperback edition.
Second edition 2018 Paperback edition.

National Library of Australia Cataloguing-in-Publication entry
Author: Iles, Helen, 1954- author.
Title: Of bushmen and brumbies : rhythms of the bush / Helen Iles.
ISBN: 9781876922665 (paperback)
Notes: Includes index.
Subjects: Australian poetry--21st century.
Dewey Number: A821.3

Linellen Press
265 Boomerang Road,
Oldbury, W.A. 6121
www.linellenpress.com.au

Dedication

This book is dedicated to all the fine horsemen and horsewomen who truly know the joys of riding behind the mob on the back of a horse in Australia's great outback, and to those who enjoy bush poetry.

Contents

Of Bushmen and Brumbies i
Dedication iii
Contents v
Acknowledgments vii
The Breaker's Walk 1
The Day the Breaker Broke 3
The Horse from Ethel Creek 6
The Polo-crosse Match 12
The Warrahben Annual Cup 17
The Stockman's Lament 24
In Yester Years 26
In The Old Days 28
Drovers' Day 29
Brave Molly 30
Comrade In Arms 33
Pioneer Days 35
Wild Horse 36
Northwest Christmas 38
In One Fowl Swoop 41
Billabong Spirit 45
Have You Ever …? 46
Kimberley Dream 49

NON-RHYMING POEMS	51
The Walers' Prayer	53
Any Place	54
Serpent River	57
About the Author	60

Acknowledgments

My sincerest thanks to my friends and family
who encouraged me to write poetry,
and to Hunter, the roguish colt,
who gave me so much to write about.
My love to you all.

The Breaker's Walk

Have you ever pondered the reasons that be
why the Breaker walks with his knees in the breeze?
Why a whole day shines through between each slender thigh?
Well I'll tell you the reason why.
But first you must note that the man isn't addled
to want to spend all his days in the saddle,
Aahh, but that's not the cause of the curve of his pants
nor the awkward bow-legged stance.

Well you've heard how the old saying goes, of course
that the wildest of colts makes the best horse
It's the Breaker's job to make that come true,
but that's not so easy to do,
for they fight and they buck and they won't give an inch
resenting the band of the hard drawn up cinch
and the Breaker must stay astride of each toss
until he has mastered the hoss.

But it sometimes occurs that a horse lands a buck
that catches the Breaker down on his luck
and strive as he may and fight as he must
eventually he will bite the dust.
But it's part of the trade to know how to fall,
tuck up the limbs in a tight curling ball,
to limit the breaks avoids full defeat,
so he lands on the flesh of his seat.

Helen Iles

Now it comes with the turf of the career he pursues
never to mention the size of the bruise
so he grins and he bears it, rubs it and then
strides back to the horse and mounts it again.
Yet he knows by the ache in his shoulder and hip
and the fresh streak of red on his blooded top lip,
that a good horse will come from this wild bucking colt,
He could tell by the hard hitting jolt.

And he knows when it's done he'll feel old for his age
and he'll mutter his curses to lessen his rage
and he'll cringe in his legs and he'll walk with disdain
and it's all on account of the pain.

Now if you've ever been launched from the back of a hoss
to land on your seat from the height of the toss,
If you've ever felt numb from the hard jarring hit,
even you might swear just a bit.

And well you might ask, how I know what I know,
well, I apprenticed the Breaker for a year or so,
I learnt full his trade and the mode of his talk,
and I mastered the bow-legged walk.

*****

The Day the Breaker Broke

There's a limit to the level
that the Breaker-man can take,
And it's not so very pleasant
when that pressure makes him break.
Now it's odd what goes occurring
when the Breaker-man has broke,
So I'll tell you all my story
if you swear I haven't spoke
Of all such things that went about
the last time he got stoked,
For it was the craziest of days,
the day the Breaker broke.

Now his bones were strong and solid,
'twas his mind that took a turn,
Too much temper bottled in him
and the Breaker finally burned,
And his yards were filled with loonies
no-one else would ever straddle,
And the rails were strewn with bridles
and the Breaker's breaking saddle.
But he stormed across the horse-yards,
his last dumping for the day,
'Twas the second time since lunchtime,
'twas the way he made his pay.

But he'd had enough this time around,
his aches were all attuned,
And he bellowed 'cross the fences,
"I'm on holidays … till June!!"
Well he caught my look of anguish
as he strode bow-legged by,
Slapping dust out of his breeches
and that dust hung in the sky,
And he shouted his instructions
as he headed for his truck,
And he cursed the roguish gelding
for it tossed a mighty buck.

"That bucking little pony
I got out there in the yard,
Send it back to where it came from,
say it wasn't very hard.
And tell that snivelling little brat
who caused the bloody vice,
That she'd better change her tactics
and treat the damn thing nice,
For when it dumps her next time
or bites her teasing brother,
Tell 'em straight, don't bring it here
'cose they deserve each other!

And the grey that's in the stable,
well there's not a hope for him,
Not while he has the bad luck
of the owner with the sin.
Tell the guy to come and ride him
and if he brings with him his wrath,
Do a favour for me sweetheart,
slip a burr beneath the cloth.
Then tell the guy he's crazy
and offer him meat fee,
And if he sells it to you,
will you save the horse for me?

Now for that bucking chestnut
that just dented all my pride,
Leave him where he is for now
for I'll be back to end the ride.
But just for now, I'm going home
to drink away the pain,
I'm getting pissed for sanity,
Screw monetary gain!"
And he cursed those bucking horses
and he blubbered as he spoke,
And that was what I saw that day,
The Day the Breaker Broke.

*****

The Horse from Ethel Creek

There's a place in the north of Australia
where horses are bred for gain,
but they breed them in the wild,
and leave for the Blacks to tame.
Now this place that's north and inland
is flat and green and vast;
it's known by most as Ethel Plain,
and there's a creek that flows right past.

Now the station owners are cluey there
and know how to make a buck,
they muster each year through to Brumby Creek,
send the catch down south by truck
where the Big Smoke riders buy them
for they know good flesh on sight –
and they train them to play Polo
for they're swift and taut with might.

Now every so often some are born
on the banks of Ethel Creek,
but they seem to be a different type
which makes their futures bleak,
for they have a reputation
of being solid, strong, but plain,
and even though they look quite grand
they're lacking half a brain.

Of Bushmen and Brumbies

Now I heard of one that had been born
right on the river's tide
and it's been professed that this big colt
even the Blacks won't ride.
They shout out loud, "Not dis pella boss,
dat bugga, him too hard."
Now I have the strangest feeling that
that bugger's in my yard.

He bucks, he rears, he bites, he kicks,
not a vice is left untested;
he gives it all with daunting strength,
much anger he has vested.
He's tough and strong, and lightning fast,
and not the slightest lazy.
In time I'd come to fear the worst,
this blighter's downright crazy.

He'd been trucked down from pastures wild,
for Polo he was destined,
but it wasn't to be – the rider wised,
and his temperament was questioned.
So they left him on, drove further south,
a pub crawl they were taking;
till late that night a drunk did buy
this 'polocrosse horse in the making'.

Now this little horse had a mind of his own
and he'd loved the open plain,
and I'm sure he'd vowed not to ever submit
to play man's silly game.
Well, to shorten the story a mile or so,
this rider soon came to me
saying, "You've got a name curing many a rogue.
Can you do this job for me?"

So I took it on, this little horse,
not knowing from whence it came;
a little horse with a wild eye
and a temper to match that acclaim.
So Billy the Black, my offsider,
led him off and away up the race,
came back and said, "Me no like dis one boss,
got a mean ole look on him face."

But I laughed, "Don't worry, Billy,
I'll do this one alone.
You've taught me much over many years,
now my knowledge is full-grown."
Well he shot me a hard look in query,
was a look that would stir the dead,
and as he shrugged and turned, I heard him say,
"And so is da boss-woman's head."

But I didn't listen to the taunt,
I rode him while Billy looked on,
and I'd never sat such a fierce ride
as I got from that son-of-a-gun.
He broke my finger, cracked a rib,
ricked my neck and blooded my lip,
but I wouldn't yield to that fiery cur,
gasped air and restructured my grip.

And I yelled to Billy to 'let him loose',
needing room to stretch his bound
- 'twas an old trick of Billy's for wilder brutes –
run them into the ground.
And when they were tired you pushed them more
to be sure of their strength being spent,
then a quiet ride home to reward them;
no more nonsense or fighting dispensed.

So out through the gate we did gallop,
and into the pine forests long,
we vanished from view in an instant,
his feet dancing out a quick song.
And onward and onward he bolted,
five mile flat strap we did race,
and I readied my spur for the moment,
and used them when he slacked the pace.

Helen Iles

Another five mile we did travel
till he shook and was heaving for air
then I gently drew rein on the bridle,
to misfit more he'd not dare.
So I turned his head back to look homeward;
the lesson full learnt to this guy,
when off he did dash in an instant;
and I knew I was going to die.

Ten mile he did bolt without lagging
his speed even greater to home
and he didn't flinch once to my pulling hands
while his mouth and body flecked foam.
Then into my vision soon entered
the homestead and yards did appear,
while I clung to my saddle, my lifeline,
my eyes and mouth wide with great fear.

He soared o'er the slip rails so spritely
while my hands made his mouth red and torn,
and I sailed o'er the gate to the garden,
landed flat on my back on the lawn.
Now Billy the black wandered over,
a grin spread from ear to ear,
he took up the reins of the mongrel
and over the gate paused to jeer.

Of Bushmen and Brumbies

"You did good, missie-boss, I can tell ya.
Him sure gotta fast way to run,
but I still say old Billy not ride him
'coz dis old black pella not dumb."
Now my head is reduced in Billy's eyes;
my pride in myself is more humble.
But it took a big toss from that wild hoss
for my self-esteem to crumble.

Well, I crawled on my knees from the lawn to the house,
and on hands pained and torn to the bone,
reached the office desk, my whole body numb,
swallowed deeply and picked up the phone;
for there's a brand on that big colt's left shoulder,
who its owner I sought information,
and I wasn't surprised when they told me
it belonged to an Ethel Creek station.

Now I wangled a deal with colt's rider
and bought the horse just the same
but took Billy's advice and promised an oath
that this horse I would never tame.
And on days when it's cold and I ache in my bones
and my fingers and neck start to creak,
I look out to the yards and remember the day
I was trounced by the horse,
          the horse from Ethel Creek.

*****

The Polocrosse Match

It was us against the Country team, the last match of the day
eight minutes to a chukka, the last one left to play.
The teams were lined up side by side,
the umpire made the toss
and started up the battle in this game of polocrosse.

For those who do not know the game I'd better just explain.
It's a bit like rich-man's Polo but just a tad the same.
Not us who hit that little ball with mallet swinging quick …
too easy, so we use device, a netted round end stick
with which we scoop and snatch the ball
from ground or in mid-air,
and heading down towards the goal
ride fast as we would dare.
And there we strive to top the score
and trounce those Pastoral fools;
while riding game and reckless, we'll even break the rules.

Our team this day had Macca and his brother Ed McLean,
who was mounted on a thoroughbred, a leggy grey that's lean
while Macca rode a donkey-type, a nag of ill-repute
that took the aptly title of 'Surreptitious Brute'.
That made up two on our side, this team that soon would be
the winners of the Championship; the lucky third was me.
And I was mounted on a cur, a chestnut half their size
but what The Hunter lacked in build, his brain did maximize.

Of Bushmen and Brumbies

The weekend fray was nearly done, the trophy in our sights -
ne'er before we'd come this far and so we'd vowed to fight.
To win the match our single aim, we pushed it to the fore,
though all of us were three parts done
from a binge the night before.
And with our trusty steeds and sticks
we'd come out on the field
to put our talents to the test, our brains still booze-congealed.

The country lads looked fresh and bold and shared an evil eye
but we sneered back with bleary orbs:
these bums were going to die!
We wouldn't let them take our prize, the trophy of the game.
This was going to be our day, our honour and our fame.
No matter what we had to do this city team would soar;
we'd not be widely known as the Losing team no more.

So here we were all ready, the ball was in the sky,
a-hovering over Eddie's head; it almost passed him by.
Racquets reached and knocked about to take hold of the toss;
we struggled hard but in the end, the spongy ball was lost.
It found the reach of Country's team and landed in the net.
The rider got away from us as fast as he could get.
He galloped down towards the goal - I needed to be quick!
The umpire wasn't looking so I hit him with my stick.

He howled with pain, he cried with rage as I picked up the ball
and tossed the thing to Eddie who off down the field he tore.
He threw for goal - a brilliant shot –
while the Country was left for dead
but it hit the post, rebounded back,
and bounced off Eddie's head.

A rustic lad reclaimed the sphere of sponge that was the ball
and didn't check his speed one bit as Eddie took a fall.
Towards his goals, he didn't veer; he bumped us in his run,
I heard The Hunter grunt in stride
and knew he'd have some fun.
The chestnut cur did slow his pace
as our rival charged on course;
and I smiled with glee as Hunter's teeth
ripped that rider from his horse.
And grinning snide, I dared to yell: 'The other team are fools'
then winced a bit on noticing the Umpire check the rules.

But Mac was quick to follow up and swiftly claimed the ball
and standing on his saddle seat gave show to one and all.
Swinging wild his racquet as he galloped boldly for'ard
the ball was launched out of the net,
and bloody hell, … we scored!

Of Bushmen and Brumbies

So back into the line-up, the ball was tossed again,
the country lads determined that our efforts were in vain.
And dirty tricks they also used to stop our deadly run;
sandwiching and bumping us … my, this game was fun!

And while we played in brilliant style, our minds stayed in a fog
encouraged more by side-line sips
of the Hair of last night's dog.
And so the minutes ticked away, the melee was full on;
the game was coming to an end as was the setting sun.
With seconds to go, the final line was straightened up for play -
the ball was snatched up instantly, the rider got away.
And down the field we chased him, racing neck and neck
till Hunter grabbed him by the leg and dropped him to the deck.

A dusty tussle started then, for the ball we had to look
while the Umpire still searched frantically
through the rules inside the book.
And while he looked the game went on,
 clouds rising from the ground
obscuring all the vision as the horses milled around.
And somewhere in that bustling crush
of legs and sticks and ball
someone tossed the sphere up and a goal was seen by all.

Helen Iles

And there the whistle sounded after scoring score for score;
the field was left a dusty place, the riders bruised and sore.
And for our toil and effort there always comes the prize;
and so we turned upon it our grateful blood-shot eyes;
stood there beside the country team,
the Goodies from the bush
and us - the cheating bastards team - stood woozy and a-flush.

And listening to the victory speech, the prize held in the air
our mouths agape and going dry
 while the band played Australia Fair.
And for the final tally …
Who scored the final toss?
Well wouldn't you know, with all our skill …
        Bloody hell, we lost!

*****

The Warrahben Annual Cup

It was Warrahben in the month of May,
time for the picnic meet.
The town was full of city folk -
it was them they had to beat
for they'd come up from the Big Smoke
in their great big flashy cars,
towing fancy horse floats
'quipped with stereos and bars.
And they'd brought up to the country
the fine thoroughbreds they prized,
making outback station nags
look somewhat undersized.
But, never mind, an oath was sworn
when they'd won the Cup last year,
that Warrahben would win it back,
of that they had no fear.
So everything was ready
for the Annual Picnic Race
and Warrahben had it all set up
to fill the major place.

Now the station nags were an ill-bred lot,
they ranged in breed and height;
up against the city steeds
they were a sorry sight.
But what they lacked in beauty,
they doubled up in heart,
and that included Crippled James,
Dust-eater and The Tart.
And one more came to Warrahben
from way out in the bush
His presence on the race track
caused a subtle hush
for his eye did glint like metal
and his coat shone fiery red
and proud he bore his rider
while aggression fuelled his tread.

Now the girl that perched upon him
was a young and slender slip
and the silks that fluttered on her back
matched the make-up on her lip.
The city jockeys chuckled
for they thought she'd lack the guts,
but she simply said "Move over, boys,
the horse I'm on is 'Nuts.'
We've come to claim the trophy,
on you his wrath he'll reek,
and I warn you not to get in his way
'cose he comes from Ethel Creek."

Then care-fully she scanned the field,
remembering all their names;
Rocketman, Insidious,
Speed Chief, Crippled James,
Apple Jack from further north,
The Demon from the south.
Then casually she re-applied
the lipstick to her mouth.
And on her right she noted
White Lightning and King Tuts,
The Tart, Dust-eater, Crowbait,
and her chestnut colt called Nuts.

And there the Starter took his place
as she took up the reins,
and took a fist for added strength
of fiery chestnut mane.
And as the gun retorted loud,
Nuts he reared up,
dumping her upon the line
at the start of the Warrahben Cup.
And over the sound of thunder
as the horses tore away
she heard the rising laughter
of the crowd who watched the fray.

But anger rose within her
as she snatched the reins again,
smarting and a-cursing
with embarrassment and pain.
And putting foot to stirrup,
she was only part astraddle
when Nuts took off to join the field
landing her behind the saddle.
And there she stayed throughout the race
a-struggling on his back
as Nuts did close the distance
to the horses on the track.

And closer, ever closer,
to the bouncing bums ahead
while hers was bruised from jolting,
all sensations going dead.
And through the field did gallop
that wretched chestnut cur,
with her behind the saddle seat
unable to whip or spur.

Then pounding mid the runners,
passing Crippled James and Tart,
Apple Jack and Rocketman
who was fuelled by a constant fart …
till neck and neck with Speed Chief
they streaked the endless mile
and as Nuts bolted to the lead
she deigned to turn and smile.

Then off towards the leaders,
it was them she had to beat
passing now Insidious,
she regained her saddle seat.
And grunting loud in anger
Nuts strived with all his might,
passed the one called Demon
and the Lightning that was white.
Dust-eater was the next to yield
to the chestnut's fiery wrath,
and the snorting roars at Crowbait's heels
made the rangy bay veer off.
And now was but just one horse left,
the foamed and frothy Tuts,
the race was now a two way thing,
just him and the fiery Nuts.

Ahead the bay did gallop,
his body white and wet,
with Nuts on his heels in hot pursuit,
he'd not yet raised a sweat.
And into view did enter
the line that signalled the end
of the Annual Warrahben Picnic Cup –
it was just around the bend.

King Tuts was racing out in front,
now soolled by the jockey's whip,
it beat a rhythmic pattern
from the shoulder to his hip.
But still the chestnut pounded out
long strides upon the track,
his rider perched in stillness,
barely moving on his back.
And 'go' she stirred him kindly,
"You darling little cur,
I have no need to whip you,
nor rake you with the spur.
Come on now, just two strides left,"
and he took her on to win,
his nose in front of King Tut's head,
his eyes and nose flaring.

And while the other riders slowed
and stopped to rest awhile
Nuts continued galloping,
he did another mile.
And while the Cup was handed
to the Mayor of Warrahben,
Nuts and his pulling rider,
they went round once again.
But her face was now a grimace,
all twisted up with pain,
as she still stood upon the irons
a-hauling on the reins.
As for the city jockeys
who had laughed when she'd arrived,
they looked quite dismal now
that of the Cup they'd been deprived.
And sitting now in their defeat
they cowered mild and meek,
as off into the scrub did fly
that Horse from Ethel Creek.

And Cup in hand, the Mayor did say –
for one and all, free beer.
And he prayed to God that pair could be found
in time for the race next year.

* * * * *

The Stockman's Lament

The camp-fire glowed red 'gainst the backdrop of night,
the sky was peppered with stars,
'neath a tree on the plain a stockman reclined,
on his jew-harp he strummed a few bars.
And he stared at the embers, his mind far away,
his aloneness irking him not,
for the dog at his feet and the horse he'd turned out
was all that a man could want.

His life as a Drover had been fairly good,
though he'd seen his fair share of bad too,
but ne'er did he grieve while his mates were afoot,
Old Plodder and dog, Jimmy Blue.
And he wondered now as he stared at the flames
as the dog rose and came to his side,
what else to do now that age was about
and he was no longer able to ride?

And what of the dog, his best friend in life,
– he'd had others; Mate, Harry and Jack -
and he remembered the pain as he'd buried each one
way out there on the overland track.
And he thought of the tears that still welled as he passed
the markers where each one did lay,
and he stroked the pup's brow and forced back the thought
that Blue too would be out there one day.

Of Bushmen and Brumbies

But the flickering flames fired other thoughts up,
a ponderance of what was ahead.
What would Blue do when it happened to pass
that he was the first to be dead?
Would Blue stay by his side, and cry at the find,
if his life passed away with the night?
Would he sit through the dark and reflect on the times
they had had till the grey early light?

And what if he did, (as he'd done in the past),
would he stay till his life too was done?
Or else pad the trails they had traveled for years,
for life forever moves on.
And staring now into Blue's worried eyes,
he stroked his best pal with old hands,
and remorsed at the thought of him dying alone,
unable to live off the land.
Or maybe he prayed, wheezing out life's last tune,
he'd join with a dingo mob …
then in sounds of the night, his eyes rolled to the sky -

He left it all up to God.

*****

In Yester Years

From distant gloom the lad doth walk,
the lantern swinging lights his way.
He huddles from wind's mournful talk
and longs for bright of day.

He makes the shed in lantern light,
its brilliance blinks up bleary eyes
which sore squint back against the bright
and stirs up sleepy sighs.

From lantern light upon the rows
on heads that turn in long maned gleam,
the Clydesdales wake to dawning glow,
lose paddocks from their dreams.

The boy then hoists the light aloft;
he hooks it up, then doles the grain;
the heads go down into the trough;
breakfast begins again.

And while the heads are drooping low,
the collars are dragged down;
he heaves them on with mighty throw
the giants with the shaggy crowns.

Of Bushmen and Brumbies

With bridles on, and collars tight,
he leads them one by one
out to dawn's first early light
and snaps the tracers on.

Wiping sleeve on sweaty brow
his task is nearly done,
he drives the twelve out to the plough
where the boss awaits the sun.

And there he hands the reins across
and, wary, snaps the plough hooks on;
the mighty horses' coats are gloss,
twelve giants lumber on.

And putting shoulder to the load
they wait there, dutiful ...
till the farmer slaps the mighty reins
and orders gruffly, Pull!!

Then pounding, hairy, giant feet
lift high with rising sun,
tremendous strength to the collar goes:
and the ploughing has begun.

******

In The Old Days

Beneath the arms of spreading tree
a child's swing hangs which once brought glee
to all the urchins, tousled heads,
playing round the shearing sheds
while high inside their fathers plied
the Tally Ho where clippers glide
through snowy bellies, deep in wool
sweeping, gliding,
till the bales were full.

And all around the laughter flowed
the banter, bleating as the fleece was mowed
the clatter of denuded sheep
upon the ramp to the holding keep below.
I still can see it so.
Though now for many years the shed is still
the laughter, banter, bleating gone – is nil.
I stand and watch the ghostly shearers stoop;
The ghostly sheep still to the shed yards troop;
the children swinging laugh in ghostly play
while I wish my life back to those glory days

*****

Drovers' Day

Across the wide vast country of mulga, dust and flies
stockmen make their campfires 'neath diamond studded skies
And stretch out on their swag rolls beneath the boab trees
To dream about those girls in town while cooled by night's soft breeze.

By day they ride their horses in the dust behind the mob
Not once ever believing there could be a better job
For soon a beast will venture to the scrub on either side
And the stock horse leaps to battle, giving man a thrilling ride.

The days are long and dusty on a stockhorse taut with pride
But nowhere would they rather be than on this cattle ride
The drives that built this nation are remembered far and wide
From up along the Birdsville Track down to the Great Divide

But then the sun diminishes behind the flat red plain
And darkness fills the western sky as evening slowly wanes
The campfire embers filter up from the resting fray
To join the glittering diamonds at the end of drovers' day.

*****

Brave Molly

Across the burning desert sands
the soldiers made their run.
The horses bravely galloping,
their coats reflecting sun
as bullets whizzed and plopped around
destroying targets large.
the soldiers ducked their heads and yelled
on the Tenth Light Horse last charge

Mick was riding on the flank,
his Molly in full flight.
His hands were trembling on the reins
when he felt the bullets bite.
The impact knocked him from his horse
with a loud resounding whack;
he hit the sand, lay deathly still
till Molly trotted back

She stood with him beneath the sun
as the battle raged around.
Her body casting shadows
over Mick upon the ground.
At times she gently nuzzled him
in asking him to rise.
And Mick looked up and blessed her,
to him she was a prize

Of Bushmen and Brumbies

He'd picked her out some months ago,
this roguish chestnut mare.
So wild of eye, she'd challenged him
to 'ride me if you dare'
They'd had some fights, some breaking of
the man, the horse and saddles.
Till one day Molly suddenly
let Mick stay full a-straddle

Until that time had happened,
her strength and courage bound
meant sometimes Mick was mounted,
the next upon the ground.
Yet something 'bout this chestnut mare,
in his heart she held the place.
'tis where he kept those cherished things,
now his fingers stroked her face

She nickered soft and deeply
as her muzzle touched his cheek
As she tried to push him upward
but he was quickly growing weak
The bullets passed right through him
and his head was pained and addled
When Molly lay beside him
to help him in the saddle

"Good on you, mate," he told her
as he barely swung astride
We may have had our differences
but, girl, you've done me proud
And up she stood with Mick aboard
and gentle made her tread
Back to the line from whence she came,
too late though – Mick was dead.

But Molly girl was treasured
for the role she played that day
in bringing home her Hero
from the sand where he had lay
A part of war-time history,
the Tenth Light Horse last run
When they charged through hails of bullets
in the desert 'neath the sun.

Comrade In Arms

Goodbye, sweet Meg, I did not see this day coming
and the pain in my heart is fiercely drumming
as my rifle, heavy, aims at your face
for I must not leave you in this wretched place.

Orders is orders, we're now going home
to the land of your birth but we must go alone
No room for our horses on the ships homeward bound
We don't understand this, their thinking ain't sound.

Strewn over beaches lie the corpses of mates
who carried us boldly at maximum gait
as they surged into battle and swept over sand
held tight to the bridle by fearful hands.

You carried us bravely, and on you we won
'cose you held tight your line and charged 'neath the guns.
and not once you faltered though bullets whizzed by
Oh my sweet Meg, I don't want you to die.

The ships are now leaving and I lower my gun
I cannot destroy you, my heart you have won
so I leave you, sweet Meg, may your life bear no pain
even though I shall never see you again.

Helen Iles

Our ships cut the waves and draw out to sea
as the horses abandoned stand watching and scream
then into the surf they plunge to the hip
and moving as one swim after the ship

We stand on the stern and pray you turn back
but the waves crash o'er you as your stride is taxed
the sea is too strong and the ship will not stop
for we have no way to get you atop

Tears fill my eyes that you cannot be saved
as I cry like a baby as you sink 'neath the waves
Each day of remembrance my face streaks with wet
as I see you so clearly, sweet Meg,
and I shall ne'er forget.

*****

Pioneer Days

The land lay open, a vast expanse,
a terrain of plateaus with gums stately stance.
with mulga and swampland and desert and plains,
scorched open by droughts then flooded by rains,
and throughout the country roved settlers in bands
forging a nation from Australia's cruel lands.

And hampered by winds, and hampered by sun,
they carved out a future then enjoyed what they'd done.
Their children now reap the rewards of their ways
yet remember not much of the Pioneer days.
And they cry and they moan at the hardships they meet
yet not once ever think of the perils their ancestors beat.

*****

Wild Horse

Windswept mane to the sky goes swirling
With dignity your strong neck's curling
Roaring snorts to the world proclaiming
Your spirit free forever.

Across the land your feet once thundered
Raiding bands, more mares you plundered
Renegade colts scarred as they blundered
For your rule was good and strong.

Body black,' neath sun it glistened
Ears alert, flicked while you listened
Didn't see the old man, wise and wizened
Nor the trap he set that day.

And though you'd led that brumby band
You bore me strongly across my land
Our friendship lost when life's cruel hand
Burnt all the fences down.

Now you're home again, though mourning capture
Your tears fall silent in the high enclosure
I long to see you, again feel your rapture
So tamed no more will you be.

Of Bushmen and Brumbies

And so my friend, the yard gate's swinging
Take your freedom now, to the bush go fleeing
Go far away from man's style of living
Go galloping wild and free.

So swiftly he went, his black mane a-flying,
Proud muscles rippling, heart gladly soaring
Freedom was his, his shrill neigh was calling
To the brumby herd he ran.

He'll die out there, I know it will happen,
He'll die in the bush, spirit freed to the heaven,
But for now he is free, Lord King of his Harem
Stallion Wild, and my friend ne'er forgotten.

*****

Northwest Christmas

It's Christmas in the North-west.
Santa's due to come,
to bring some prezzies for the kids,
and some for Dad and Mum,
but we never listen for his bells
for his reindeer he ain't got.
He cannot bring them with him
'cose the sand's too bloody hot.

So he comes by flying camel
and he comes in shorts and thongs,
says they're cooler in the desert
while he sings his Santa songs,
and he Ho Ho Ho's as usual
though his beard is white with zinc.
He's a strange one, our old Santa,
if you ask me what I think.

Well he came this year to our town,
a day early he arrived,
and he wandered off the desert
looking more dead than alive.
He was sorry to come early
from his parched throat he did bark,
but he had to do a day shift
'cose his camel hate the dark.

Of Bushmen and Brumbies

Well he looked about forlornly
while a tinny he did crack,
not another word he uttered
while he knocked the whole thing back
Then he sadly said he's sorry;
the gifts he'd bought for all our fun --
he couldn't give them to us now
for they'd melted in the sun.

But he looked upon our anger
and said he felt a fool,
how about then for our pleasure
if he gave the town a pool?
for it's stinking in the North-west
and there's not a place to swim;
no water left upon the ground
for cooling heated limbs.

So we said, 'Yes, thank you, Santa,'
as he knocked his third brew back,
and he grabbed another dozen up,
staggered off down the desert track.
Well we woke next day, 'twas Christmas;
looked out to our Town Pool at dawn;
shook our head in awe at our Santa,
saw the kids all looking forlorn.

Helen Iles

Now we know old Santa is senile
and the kids now think he's a pain;
if we want to swim in the Town Pool,
      it looks like we must now pray for rain.

*****

In One Fowl Swoop

It was hiding in the stables, it was lurking in the dark;
the cat had run for cover far away.
It had scared off all the children while the dog in fear did bark
the crowd hung back to watch the bloody fray.

Now the job for James was simple - to bed down all the cattle,
but the rooster had the stables in his clasp,
and he would let none enter without a raging battle
in which he clawed and spurred all in his grasp.

So all outside stood wary just a-listening to its broooook
for they knew the red-eyed fowl was fighting wise
and none would venture forward to oust the evil chook
for its beak and spurs were lethally oversized.

So they gathered full of interest for the night was growing dim,
and they pondered how to force this chook's edict
so James could bed the cattle though his temper now was slim
so evict they must this fearless red-eyed chick.

Now James said they could blast it out and went and got his gun
He filled its chambers full of buckshot lead
and fired fifty cartridges then deemed the job was done
while smoke wafted through the slug holes in the shed.

Then James did staunchly enter the rooster's hazy lair
to find the body riddled with his shot
and he screamed and yelled and hollered, ran back fast he dare
for he'd not hit the thing he'd thought he'd shot.

His skin was ripped to pieces, his face was pale with fright
he said it fought him like the very dickens;
and he swore it laid in ambush just beyond the shaft of light
and now he feared that rampant red-eyed chicken.

But James's courage lifted and he strode ahead again,
this time an axe was hanging from his hand
He'd kill the evil Rhode Isle for the terror it instilled;
he'd show he was undaunted by its stand.

So he swung the axe head swiftly, he swung with all his might
but all his efforts proved to be in vain
for no matter how he flailed it while suffering fowlish spite
he failed to clear the rooster's night domain.

"That does it," Jimmy shouted, still licking at his pride
"You're day is up you wretched violent chook!"
He edged back to the doorway with the hose to make a tide
and snuck another stealthful worried look.

Dashing at the opening with the fire hose full on
he flooded every stall and ceiling raft
and he laughed as water geysered through the gunshot holes he'd made
as rats and water poured out fore and aft.

And he danced and laughed maniacally and gaily leapt around
as he flooded all the stables inside out
as he yelled enthusiastically "Drown you bugger, drown."
as he waited for the chook to be washed out.

Then we listened so intently as the silence slowly grew,
as the dark and quiet stables showed James' luck,
and were just about to pat him on the back as he was due
when we heard the paltry poultry's gentle brooook.

So James acquired some matches and piled wood by the door
He lit the wood and watched the flames arise
and he laughed aloud and shouted as the shed in fire did raze
while a maniacal look blazed in his eyes.

And while giving a new meaning to hot Red Rooster chicken
he watched the shed come crashing to the ground
and he cheered so exuberantly that he'd sent chook to the dickens
as that shed set fire to all the sheds around.

And through the smoke a red-combed bird went off in a flurried rush
seeking cooler climates nearby
while James did realise slowly what he'd done and went aflush
for the flooding hose had bled the wells all dry.

Next morning came,
and James in sleep did smile that flames were gone
but the stable ruin meant so now was his job
and he thought of what's important, and the vision lingered long
as he felt that all his wounds were now a-throb.

Yet he smiled again at winning, at the death of Brewster's reign
but it faded as the daylight rose anew
for that vengeful Rhode Isle rooster struck a chord with sheer disdain
and let out a curdling Cock-a-doodle-doo!

*****

Billabong Spirit

White teethed children, black faces gleam
frolic in water 'neath Coolibah stream
watched by old women and young bucks fishing
when they noticed a small piccaninny was missing

'Where is Imgali?' the old ladies cried
Rods dropped to the banks as the young bucks tried
to find young Imgali, the youngest tribe daughter,
Three searched the bushes, two dived into water.

'She been playing by wet logs,' one child called out
'I see'd her in water there splashin' about.
She be laughin' and squealin' just moments ago
But where she gone now ... oh hell ... I dunno.'

Young bucks dropped to coolness, line breasted the water
soon pulled up the body of tribe's youngest daughter
'Imgali! Imagali!' the old ladies screamed.
The kids all forbid now to swim in the stream.

And the young bucks no longer can dangle their line
lest they bring up her spirit with Barra entwined
Yet they sit on the rocks there and solemnly wish
as they watch her swim naked – Imgali, the fish.

*****

Have You Ever ...?

Have you ever heard a kookaburra laugh
from gum trees high on a shimmering plain?
Have you ever copied a kangaroo's bound
going boing, boing, boing again and again?

Have you ever stroked a bobtail's scales -
kept your fingers away from its teeth so small?
Have you felt the skin of a gecko's stub tail;
seen it shrink from you so tall?

Have you ever cradled a bat in your hands
beneath an old fruit tree?
Its silky fur through your fingers glide,
a delight to you and me.

Have you ever sat and enjoyed this place,
the sounds and smell of the land;
felt a glowing gold sun warm on your face
as red dust sifts through your hand?

Have you ever dabbled your feet in the cool
at a billabong deep in the bush,
with a friend by your side smiling wider than wide
while your laughter disturbs the still hush?

Have you ever moved cattle along a red track
riding high on your Dad's big grey horse
with Dad right before you, his hat shading yours? –
Oh, my Dad's a stockman, of course.

Have you ever slept out under starlit skies,
heard magpies chortle at dawn
to rouse sleepy heads to a smoky dim day? –
You raise your head with a yawn.

Have you ever felt pleased at the cattle drive's end
when you see your Mum on the verandah?
You slide from the rump, take your Dad's sweaty reins
and across to the stockyards meander.

Have you ever felt pleased as your Dad stands so proud
watching you pad rough through the dust?
And you kick at a rock and smile to yourself
– to feel this way is a must.

Well I've stood at the gate in the late afternoon
looking out to the plains wide and red.
The dog at my side is as happy as I
as I reach down and pat his broad head.

And the sounds of the birds cackling high in the trees
make me know this land is not alien
as I watch the 'roos bound and the fruit bats fly free …
Gee, I'm glad I'm Australian.

*****

Kimberley Dream

To wake in my swag with a wide stretching yawn
and be gently caressed by a Kimberley dawn
in a camp that I pitched by a cold rippled stream
is only a part of my Kimberley dream.

White birds overhead that are bickering anew
wing far far away in the Kimberley blue,
to where cockatoos rest in Albizia trees
make my memories soar on the Kimberley breeze
to when crouched round a fire in a mustering camp
huddling to keep warm in the Kimberley damp;
of lying flat out on a pool crystal deep
soothing the skin in the Kimberley heat.
of droving the cattle across the vast plain
or cleansing the skin in the Kimberley rain
or when stepping to ground from a horse that I trust
to sink my feet deep in the Kimberley dust.

When I left this land long time my heart sorely hurt
till I lay my swag back in the Kimberley dirt
In the Kimberley sun or the Kimberley flood
the life in this land is my Kimberley blood.
And now in my swag watching black clouds form
I know it's the first of the Kimberley storms

Helen Iles

The changes are coming, no seasonal regret
its time for the winter – the Kimberley wet
when rainfall eradicates land's steamy haze
giving relief from hot Kimberley days
where far and wide such magnificence seen
rolls on and on in new Kimberley green.

After droving long years in this glorious land
I'll give my bones up to the Kimberley sand
To die in the top-end's a sure-fired must
so my soul can drift on in the Kimberley dust

And now that I've lived to life's journey's end
I let my soul fly on the Kimberley wind
I lie on my swag as life passes me by
'neath a boab tree 'neath a star-filled Kimberley sky

*****

NON-RHYMING POEMS

The Walers' Prayer

Bless you, oh gallant steed
for you will carry our heroes far
May your sure feet and bold heart
carry you safe across the battle lines.
Winged be your spirit
and may our Lord protect you from all harm.

May you stay forever stalwart
your heart valiantly striving
though the sand be deep
and the rivers dry
and the sun beat harsh upon your skin

May your rider be kind
and gentle hands comfort you at the end of day
May the wrath of our enemies never reach your back
nor scar your soul

Stay safe oh bravest of hearts
Bring our heroes safely home again.

*****

Any Place

You stand
red dusty clothes piled high in arms too young,
skinny legs straddling cracked verandah boards
as you stare across a Namatjira scene
where orange, ochre and gold sprawls to horizon's shimmer
broken only by glistening ghost gums
and dead dry gullies.

You listen
as a young crow plays with its language
strives for perfection in the lingering stillness
as you pad to the pump
The tumult of water pounding into battered buckets
transports you to crystal clear pools
where you frolic near thrumbling cascades
tumbling down a distant gorge
the sound takes you to any place but here.

You trip
barefoot to the copper
each muddy splatter conjures cloud filled skies
damp nardhu fields
and fat sleek brown cattle
as you plunge dusty moleskins, denim blue shirts, bandanas
scrub until the froth turns red,
the water liquid mud
then you dunk with disillusionment

Of Bushmen and Brumbies

Under an angry sun
you hang half people shapes
go back inside to burgeon your dreams with far distant places
places Grandpa painted in words
while you studied his face for the truth
but his face is like a roadmap of the places he's been,
each deep crevice swelling your mind with grand possibilities.

Outside the windmill sings –
like Dame Nellie Melba, grandpa says –
and you rush in desperation
shriek as a red cloud pirouettes the garden
jigs with faded moleskins;
jives with lazy shirt sleeves
waltzes along the fence that rolls forever.
Its howl bids you follow
invites you to places you've dreamt of
to London
where ladies dress in fine lace and feathers
walk on needle heels
drink tea with elevated pinkies
talk in rounded vowels you sometimes practice.

Jostled by the dust swirl the crow flies off to a ghost gum
as you tear down your efforts
stomp inside and sweep the paddock from the table
fold red dusty clothes
as you wish for black cockatoo skies,
a screeching Nellie Melba
mud pouring from the roof top
flooded nardhu fields
and market fat brown cattle

But all you hear is the mournful *aaaaah* from a treetop
And know it's the sound of lonely

*****

Serpent River

Rain trickles down
wetting corrugations
dampening red earth
smothering the dust.
Black feet patter as the sky darkens
White grins brighten
as children dressed as punk rockers squeal and laugh
Dogs shake mangy coats now moist with nature's gift
And a cat slinks under the verandah

Beyond the camp
beneath a pregnant boab
elders sit
palms outstretched to the wet
as old eyes narrow.
They rise as one from the riverbank
move back to the humpy
gather up belongings from this belonging place.

The sky now rumbles
as old men gather women
quieten the children
move aside the dogs
and take their place heading for the bush.

Soon the serpent spirit will rise
overtake the river
overtake the land
move them on to new places
move them into new times.
Time has spoken of journey's need.

They will return when the bush returns
when the Serpent spirit births new places further on
when his presence no longer lingers on the land
when the wet is over.

*****

Other titles by this Author:

Writing Poetry – Simplified

Penny's Silver Dragon

We Are Different, You and I

Bitter Comes the Storm

Indelible Ink

Fire in the Heartland

The Horse Keepers

About the Author

Perth author Helen Iles is a horse breaker and trainer when not writing prose or poetry. Many of these poems were composed from her personal experiences as a horse rider and trainer over many years and during her travels through the outback.

In this collection of poems *The Horse From Ethel Creek* was awarded the ABC's State Country Session Poetry Prize; *The Breaker's Walk* received a highly commended certificate at the Grenfell Henry Lawson Festival of Arts; *Any Place* received a Commended Award in the Ethel Webb Bundell Literary Awards and *Kimberley Dream* gained a Special Mention in the Bronze Quill SWW-WA Awards.

*****

www.ingramcontent.com/pod-product-compliance
Lightning Source LLC
Chambersburg PA
CBHW071124030426
42336CB00013BA/2193